praise for *bone*

"yrsa daley-ward's *bone* is a symphony of breaking and mending. this whole book is an ache. and a balm. daley-ward effortlessly mines the bone. the diamond from the difficult. the things that are too bright and taboo. she lays her hands on the pulse of the thing. and gives wide air to the epic realities of women. the unfamiliar. the familiar. sexuality. poverty. sex work. sadness. joy. damage. and restoration. assigning them all the grace. all the nurturing. and all the love they deserve. an expert storyteller. of the rarest. and purest kind—daley-ward is uncannily attentive and in tune to the things beneath life. beneath the skin. beneath the weather of the everyday. her poetry and prose are intimate and distant. sonorous and staunch. delicate and metal. unwilling to yield and wondrously supple. daley-ward's extraordinary talent. ability. to both see and write the veins of the true life. the true lives. is a gift. a breath."

—nayyirah waheed, author of *salt.* and *nejma*

"[Yrsa Daley-Ward] is at the realm of a new wave of contemporary poets who inspire an unprecedented level of empathy and accessibility through their honest and raw approach. . . . [A] powerful collection of a woman facing tumultuous inner and external battles head-on, delivered with a hard-hitting directness, yet with inflections of optimism throughout that are bound to touch readers to their core."

—*i-D* Magazine

"The actor, author, model, and poet draws from her own experiences as well as issues affecting today's society throughout her work and is truly a storyteller ('some tall, some dark') of the soul."

—*POPSUGAR*

PENGUIN BOOKS

bone

Photo: Kirill Kozlov

Yrsa Daley-Ward is a writer and poet of mixed West Indian and West African heritage. Born to a Jamaican mother and a Nigerian father, Yrsa was raised by her devout Seventh-Day Adventist grandparents in the small town of Chorley in the North of England. She splits her time between London and Los Angeles.

Kiese Laymon is the author of a critically acclaimed novel, *Long Division*, and a collection of essays, *How to Slowly Kill Yourself and Others in America*. He has two books forthcoming: *Heavy*, a memoir, and *And So On*, a novel.

bone

WITHDRAWN
YRSA DALEY-WARD

penguin books

PENGUIN BOOKS

An imprint of Penguin Random House LLC
375 Hudson Street
New York, New York 10014
penguin.com

Original edition published by the author 2013
This edition with additional poems and a foreword by Kiese Laymon
published in Penguin Books 2017

"it is what it is" and "some kind of man" first appeared in
On Snakes and Other Stories, published in 2013 by 3:AM Press.

LIBRARY OF CONGRESS CATALOGING-IN-PUBLICATION DATA
Names: Daley-Ward, Yrsa.
Title: Bone / Yrsa Daley-Ward.
Description: New York : Penguin Books, 2017.
Identifiers: LCCN 2017031004 (print) | LCCN 2017031016 (ebook) |
   ISBN 9780525504528 (ebook) | ISBN 9780143132615 (paperback)
Classification: LCC PR6104.A456 (ebook) |
   LCC PR6104.A456 A6 2017 (print) | DDC 821/.92—dc23
LC record available at https://lccn.loc.gov/2017031004

Printed in the United States of America
10 9 8 7 6 5 4 3 2

Set in Adobe Garamond Pro
Designed by Elke Sigal

because writing is a soft and a hard place,
all at once.

contents

foreword

but that

When I was eleven years old, I was sent to stay with Grand-mama in Forest, Mississippi, for the third time because Mama didn't know what to do with me. After church, Grandmama told me to write a response, no doubt Jesus-fearing, to what she called the "Book of Poetry" in the Bible. The "Book of Poetry" was really the Book of Psalms, specifically Psalms 23:5.

> You prepare a table before me
> in the presence of my enemies.
> You anoint my head with oil;
> my cup overflows.

"Dear Grandmama," I wrote, "I do not know who 'you' is in this poem or why they would prepare a table for me if my enemies were watching when they know good and well that enemies will eat all the food off your table. I do not know why they want my head to be greasy or my cup to overflow on your carpet either unless they want me to get a whupping. But that last line does sound good compared to the whole poem."

Grandmama told me that my breakdown of the "Book of Poetry" was shameful, but she encouraged me that day to write my own poems. I filled long yellow legal pads with boastful verses about my how my adolescent fatness was the new fineness and girls who didn't recognize the new "fineness" must have been an old kind of "mindless." I started trying to write my own version of love poetry to the same imaginary mindless young woman.

But three years later, I found and obsessed over the brilliance of subject-verb disagreements in the fortunes of fortune cookies. Four years later, I found and obsessed over the "wait a minute" truths of horoscopes. Six years later, I found and obsessed over the sustained jerky exploration of the essay. Eight years later, I found and obsessed over the importance of dramatic irony in unreliably narrated short stories. Ten years later, I found and obsessed over the magic of multiple narrative threads in the novel.

Thirty years later, I was given *bone*.

But that.

bone works forward and backward, alerting me of yesterday and reminding me of tomorrow. *bone* is the fortune, horoscope, essay, short story, and novel we all want to write, and all hope to have written to us. At the end of the piece "Poetry," Yrsa Daley-Ward writes,

> The bruising will shatter.
> The bruising will shatter into
> black diamond.
> No one will sit beside you in class.
> Maybe your life will work.
> Most likely it won't at first
> but that
> will give you poetry.

By the time *bone* was given to me, I'd written ten thousand sentences, hundreds of thousands of words, two books, three unpublished manuscripts, but somehow, some way, I'd forgotten that all along I'd been given poetry thirty years earlier.

I'd been given poetry at twelve when Grandmama read my poem about my experiences with sexual abuse. When I got off my knees praying with her that night, I watched the back of Grandmama's sixty-one-year-old body heave in, pause, and heave out. When I finally placed my thumb lightly on the small of Grandmama's back, and she jerked forward and clenched the covers tighter around her body, she gave me poetry.

But that.

I'd been given poetry at sixteen when all I could think to do was steal all the wheat bread, white bread, cinnamon rolls, pitas, and hot dog buns from the bread truck after the Rodney King verdict.

But that.

I'd been given poetry at seventeen when I heard Mama tell someone on the other end of the phone that being alive was harder than she thought.

But that.

I was given poetry when I'd starved and run myself from a 319-pound heavy black boy to a 161-pound skinny black man. But that heart, and those bones, were the same. Poetry was lodged in the memory, and the memory was lodged in the bone.

Yrsa Daley-Ward makes all of us, and all of our different sensibilities, know that bruises give you poetry, and we give you poetry, and you give we poetry, and loveliness gives you poetry, and first days give you poetry, and warnings give you poetry, and emergencies give you poetry, and bones, bones have no choice but to give us poetry.

The trick is to accept what's offered.

Kiese Laymon
June 2017

bone

intro

I am the tall dark stranger
those warnings prepared you for.

emergency warning

You are one of those people, it is
clear, who needs help. I think you
should stop speaking in a low attractive
voice whenever you call. Stop
making me think of velvet and
fragrant tobacco and that first sip
of bourbon. Stop inciting
stirrings, movements between us,
little rebellions, causing chaos in all
of my darker places. The top half of
my body is at gross political warfare
with the lower. One part of me is
roaring and the other wholly
disapproves. You are a beautiful
danger. Do not force me to
open up. Some books are bound
tightly for years for reasons. Some
books are burned for their own
good, Love. Stop wearing clothes the
way that you do. Don't allow them to
cling to your body like that. Do not
follow these effortless fashions where
everything looks just so, because,
really . . . who could resist
such a thing? The Lord knows you
are beautiful and unfair. I think perhaps

you should spare a thought, dear, for those
who are sick over you, burning up with
you, damp with you. You know what you
do. You're a slow fever. Don't be so very
engaging, amusing or witty or bright.
You are causing confusion and jams in
tight spaces. You are an accident in
waiting. The type of accident with
casualties spanning from me to you and
here to there, a potential tragedy, a
stunning unborn disaster. Should I touch
you, I will suffer and you will suffer and
she will suffer. You are a danger zone. I
must not enter. I should not enter.
But I might.

liking things

Women who were brought up devout
and fearful
get stirred, like anyone else.
Want men. Want
other women. Stink under the arms at the end of
the day.
Get that all too familiar mix of fear and discontent
in the night. Want to do the things
that they Must Not Do.
Those dirty, bloody attractive things.

a fine art

You may have learned from your
mother or any other hunted woman.
Smiling at devils is a useful,
learned thing.
Swallowing discomfort down in
spades
holding it tight in your belly.
Aging on the inside only.
Keeping it forever sexy.

bone

From One
who says, "Don't cry.
You'll like it after a while."

And Two who tells you thank you
after the fact and can't look at your face.

To Three who pays for your breakfast
and a cab home
and your mother's rent.

To Four
who says,
"But you felt so good
I didn't know how to stop."

To Five who says giving your body
is tough
but something you do very well.

To Six
Who smells of tobacco
and says, "Come on, I can feel that
you love this."

To those who feel bad in the morning
yes,

some feel bad in the morning

and sometimes they tell you
you want it
and sometimes you think that you do.

Thank heavens you're resetting
ever
setting and
resetting.

How else do you sew up the tears?

How else can the body survive?

this was the story

This was the story according to her, but then she could never be trusted. It was safe to say that we had established this by now.
We had established this on a very regular basis.

On this particular morning, her story and its various possibilities did corroborate with stories she had told before, but everything else was out of sorts.
We were drinking whisky on two stools by the window.
It was freezing cold and the moon was a tiny slip of a thing in the sky.

She had woken me up for school far too early or far too late again. Also, we were trying to avoid the view.
She was house-proud but not at all garden-proud and the garden was an embarrassment, even at the wrong, pitch-black time of day.
Now she was saying that she met my father somewhere on a large boat. She was working on the Gold Leaf Cruise liner in nineteen eighty-four. The way she put it, I could be the child of one of four, possibly five, but the fifth was not likely due to timing and the fact that they were interrupted before the Point of No Return.

However, as she put it
(and never tactfully enough)
accidents do happen.

So here were the four, plus the very slim
possibility.

1. The Captain's mate

2. The dark-skinned man behind the
   bar, or

3. his friend, or

4. his other friend . . . owing to the
   fact that it had been a crazy night
   in the middle of a set of six lost,
   crazy months and she was

   a) going through a great deal.
   Heartbreak, namely

   b) drinking far too much far too
   often.

   Furthermore, she did not
   subscribe to the theory of
   regretting anything. If she did,
   she might regret not having more
   control over the situation. Also,
   most cases like this won't stand
   up in court.

5. (Least likely)
    The One she loved.

I felt that I should get up (although you couldn't
stand up to your full height in our house—do I
call it a house?)
and make a point about going to school, because
she was likely to forget.
"Anyway," she went on. "This fettered concept
of motherhood is outdated. You can go and come
back and go and come back and I shall always be
here. I shall always be here. That is real Love for
you, and don't let anyone tell you any different."

Then she began to speak in a different language.
Her lover was fast asleep in the bed, too far gone
to move. He had been sick on the pillow and was
drawing some very unsettling snores but as always
she was in her own space, not hearing.
She rested her head on the table and disappeared,
as usual.
I put on my coat, looked over them both and left
for school, or something like it.

When I came back, our house was gone.
Sometimes exactly what you want not to
happen happens anyway.

battle

Loving someone who hates
themselves
is a special kind of violence.
A fight inside the bones.
A war within the blood.

when it is but it ain't

Some of us love badly. Sometimes the love is the type of love that implodes. Folds in on itself. Eats its insides. Turns wine to poison. Behaves poorly in restaurants. Drinks. Kisses other people. Comes back to your bed at four a.m. smelling like everything outside. Asks about your ex. Is jealous of your ex. Thinks everyone a rival. Some of us love others badly, love ourselves worse. Some of us love horrid, love beastly, love sick, love anti light. Sometimes the love can't go home at night, can't sleep with itself, cannot contain itself, catches fire, destroys the belly, strips buildings, goes missing. Punches. Smashes heirlooms. Tells lies. The best lies. Fucks around. Writes poems, impresses people. Chases lovers into corners. Leaves them longing. Seasick. Says yes. Means anything but. Tricks the body. Kills the body. Dances wild
and walks away, smiling.

skill

I am my own father
but that wasn't always clear.
I had to learn my duties, fast.
It wasn't easy.

I got some lines on my face
I got a battle with the booze.
I look prettier than I am,
but there's a talent to that.

you don't know the half of it

According to you,
people like me
shouldn't go into places like this or
be around people like these
but you don't know the half of it.
The brightest of stars, frankly,
are just a load of hot air and
diamonds, sadly,
were just formed from dust and rock
and the butterfly,
remember,
used to crawl on its belly
and tiny legs
through the dirt.

secret

It has been going on like this
for years. I provide the bed
and all of my body.
She provides the drink,
foots all of the bill.

community

They say women are gentler, treat
each other better.
Please.
As if we never learned to eroticize our
rage,
to block out the screaming of the gut.

the not quite love

I haven't been home in nearly two
weeks.
My new lover has a fridge full of beer
and can almost make jollof rice
also the sex is good
and we are falling into something we
will soon mistake for love

anyway,
"home" is a problem. There are the
bills and there
are the mice
plus
there is that feeling you get
when you catch up with yourself.

lesson

The difference between attraction
and compatibility

how it kicks you in the belly every
now and then.

artichokes

Until you have been the last ones
sitting in the café on the corner and
she has kissed the dark rum from the
rim of your glass and schooled you in
the art of eating artichokes

until then,
you are not yet woman.

Until you put soft leaf to lip
touch tongue to flesh,
bite the lobe,
swallow the juice
she says will purify you
until you open it up, sigh at the color,
see its very middle and learn what
fingers are best at

until you reach further still
into that thick, hot heart
life has not yet started.

Before you had been promised.
Before she is a liar.
Before you are dismantled, fixed and
broke again you are not yet a lover.

Remember on the right night and
under the right light
any idea can seem like a good one
and love
love is mostly ill-advised but always
brave.

The most important thing to do is
not to worry. The lines on your face
will never stop the sun from coming
up. Your tears cannot affect the
weather. There are wars going on.
The one in your body is the only one
you can be sure of losing
or winning, then losing again.

You drink more water than rum these
days, don't you?
But you drink to her memory, don't
you?
And you only take artichokes in salad.
Never whole.
Not in a café on a dusky street at
midnight.
Not with her.
Never with her, or anyone like her.

heat

I miss you in tiny earthquakes
in little underground explosions
my soil is a hot disaster
Home is burning.
You're a lost thing.

relief

Thank Goodness I have nearly unlearned
folding my desire into itself
being afraid to claim it.

the good work

I was raised pulling food
out of earth. I know where
joy comes from
and how to make it.

a test—things our bodies have been

A bargaining tool
Breakfast
Confused
Developed (over)
Expensive
Fun
Ghost
Health
Igloo . . .
(Joke.)
Kissed
Lover
Mine?
Not
Offering
Pricey
Quiet, queer
Reward
Supple.
Tempting.
Undone.
Very.
Weapon
XXX
Yours (or that's what we told you).
Zest.

girls

Chinazo's married boyfriend
wants all of her friends and it isn't
as though she doesn't know it.

Oh well, she says, men will always
want to play around. He likes you.
Thinks you're sexy. How about it?

I say
it isn't my thing. She
starts laying into me,
asking me who I think I am
how can I act so high and mighty

when *everyone* knows what I am.
Everyone knows it.

I see her fixed on nails/her brittle
life/her plastic hair/her stretched-out
love/her painted lips/her bleach-red
skin

and cry a little
all the way home.

sthandwa sami (my beloved, isiZulu)

In the early hours of this morning it
was far too hot for anyone to sleep.
You told me I was strange and kissed
me
sunk your teeth into my soft bottom
lip, twice. So hard I thought you drew
blood.
I keep getting the feeling that if you
look at me for long enough
you may see that I have a thousand
fears
just like your mother who never really
wanted you to leave
meanwhile *mina* I am catching up on
the sleep that we missed
and waiting patiently to feel normal
again.
My thoughts about you are
frightening but precise.
I can see the house on the hill where
we grow our own vegetables out back
and drink warm wine out of jam jars
and sing songs in the kitchen until the
sun comes up
wena
you make me feel like myself

again. Myself before I had any solid
reasons to be anything else.
Last night you gave me space to
dream bigger than the single bed.
You laughed in your sleep and I cried
in mine
and this afternoon we might be tired
because the sun is fierce today
and so much happened between
midnight and now
but *Bhabha* you are terror and
brilliance
so
I am the kind of woman who is
already teaching my body to miss
yours
without craving.
I am the type of woman who is
already teaching my heart to miss
yours
without failing
and I am quite sure that you will find
this unnecessary
but I am already searching for a place
to run to and hide when you say,

Uthando lwami. I'm ready. Are you?

You know that I would gladly drive
with you to the other side of the

world with only the clothes I am
wearing
and the loose change
and empty peanut shells in my purse
kodwa
every time you leave the room I
worry
and think that perhaps I have
imagined you
and maybe you have imagined me.

she puts cinnamon on tomatoes

You knew you liked her when
she was talking about her life one day
and in the street the drunk women
were fighting
and the young men were playing
house music
and there were Muslims praying
amidst all this
and the taxis were honking their
horns all around her in a circle of
chaos

so she went back inside in all her
calm

and where the two of you are now, in
a different town
and different time, there are dogs
barking outside
and you love the way
her name feels behind your mouth.

She puts cinnamon on tomatoes
white pepper on carrots
mustard seeds on unlikely things
and takes wine and ice with breakfast.

She sits awake at night
and dreams with open eyes
so you are not afraid to tell her
every time you want to run.

There was a time when fingers on
white walls made you nervous
a time when you didn't pray so much
a time when you worried about what
the men in the street had to say

a time when you weren't yourself
they tell you you're an abomination to
God
how so? You speak to God more
often now
than ever before.

She sketches jellyfish
and planets
smokes a broken white pipe
and you feel like an instrument
that she's had for years.

You pool pennies together
for dinner, most nights
but you're happy.
You are. You're happy.

I'll admit it, I'm drawn to the wolves

I like the lines you use on me
they crackle a little, like magic.

I cannot pull my mind off you
even though
I do not trust your hands.

there will always be your heart

Do not shout for silence
do not shout too loud
there will always be birds outside a closed
window
a car door shutting in the next street
fine raindrops,
whispers
footsteps in puddles
some couple somewhere
having an argument
he's telling her to shut up
she's crying
threatening to leave
he's saying he doesn't give a fuck.
Do not shout for silence
do not shout too loud
there will always be
loose change spilled on a pavement
a plastic bag dancing somewhere in the
wind,
a tree stretching when it thinks no one is
there.

There will always be everything that you
mean but do not say
when I ask you what I've done to make

you so angry
and the look you give me when I've
said too much in front of our friends.

Do not go too far for peace and quiet
do not run too far
because the country can be as loud as the city
too noisy in its stillness
and anyway,
there will always be your breath
which, hard as you try,
you can't do without
you can't run away from.
There will always be your heart
beating
stronger and louder
the harder, the further
you run.

legacy

Being married was hard on my throat,
said he.
Being held
was tight round my neck.
Look, I still bear the marks,
said he.
Listen, I still can't breathe.

I've been owned for centuries,
said he.
It is love. But I will not stay.
My father
was a long dark fairy tale too.
It is and
it will be that way.

it is what it is

I saw Dad for the last time one hour
and forty-seven minutes ago, when I
took one final look at the body in the
open casket. His complexion was
dull. It looked just like him. Grayed
hair, broad nose, black lips.
His expression solemn, as it was in
life. He never smiled at us.

The church deaconess was in my ear,
going on and on about how good he
always looked in a trilby, asking what
would become of his collection,
especially the navy one with the pink
felt ribbon. I promised to be sure to
contact her and agreed that the
church was a great place for charity to
begin. She wanted to know what I
was going to do with his good winter
coat and green cashmere sweater.
Mentioned that her son and my
father probably wore the same size.

Mrs. Harrison has always been
tactless. Ever since I was little she has
gotten away with it because she is one
of the elder members of the church.

When Lemar Campbell died of a
brain tumor, Mrs. Harrison asked Lemar's
mother right at the graveside
for his walking stick. Just as they were
singing "Shall We Gather at the River"
and sprinkling the first shovel of dry
earth onto the casket. It had been a
beautiful, very ornate walking stick
with a gold handle and tip, but still.

I am tired all the time lately, but am not
sleeping. When I do, I have
strange dreams in which neither of
my parents are dead and they are
both shouting over each other,
pleading with me, trying to make
amends.
"One at a time," I say to them,
feigning exasperation, but secretly
glad of the attention.
"Calm down, both of you. One at a
time."

This. This is what happened. I still
can't believe it
but it is what it is.

The sermon drew to a close.
The final hymn was sung and the
minister urged us all to give our

hearts to Jesus. We said a prayer and
a stream of people were filing
towards the front to pay their last
respects to my father when Levy goes
over and spits in the coffin. Then
turns and walks straight out of
church, straight down the middle
aisle, casual as anything. I ran out
after Levy. He was my ride back to
London and there was nothing else I
could do for my father anyway.

We sped off outside the church in his
white BMW. We didn't speak.

We are on our way back to London.
For some reason, I keep thinking
back to the time when Dad kicked us out.
Two days later, Mum found a cheap flat up
North for us to stay in. It was mid-
March and just after my sixth birthday.
Levy and I discovered that we
had mice in the kitchen.
(Actually they were rats, but it was
nicer for us to pretend they were
mice.)
Soon after that, we became aware of
a ripe, sickly smell around the place
and we were taken away from our
mum six months later. My brother

was to go and live with our uncle
Terry in South East London and I
was to live with my Great Aunt Delle
in St. Anne's, Lancashire. No one told
us anything further than that.

When Levy and I were separated I
didn't know what to do with myself.
He was at a different school now and
he'd started to speak differently on
the phone. He told me he had a Nike
logo cut into his hair and one ear
pierced. He said he had a lot of
friends.
I didn't have much in the way of
friends and I missed him terribly.
Aunt Delle never allowed me to go
anywhere after school. We went to
church on a Saturday. I couldn't go
to sleepovers and had never been to
the cinema (Aunt Delle believes that
picture houses are an abomination). I
learned to quote the Bible inside out.
Sometimes children from school
would be shopping with their parents
on a Saturday and see all of us from
church singing in the market square and
trying to convert passersby.
People laughed at us when we tried to
tell them the Good News or hand out
tracts about the second coming of
Jesus.

It sounded as though Levy was having lots of fun in London. I tried my best to match him with made-up stories of what I was up to in Lancashire, besides eating rice and peas every night and reading the Bible out loud while Aunt Delle nodded off by the fire. Once I told him that Aunt Delle had slipped in the bath and almost broke her back and I had put her in the recovery position and alerted the authorities and was going to receive a medal the following Sunday at the Town Hall. Levy was impressed but Uncle called back, asking questions. When I was found out I got a good beating and was made to read the Bible upstairs all week and do chores. I was thoroughly miserable at the idea that my brother would think me a fraud.

The next time he called, I had been crying, because I had lost my Bible and Aunt Delle told me that I would never get to heaven if I continued to be so messy. Levy made me feel better by explaining that lost items were all due to crazy science, so it

couldn't have ever been avoided.
"It's all about entropy," he explained.
"The more energy something has, the
higher the entropy—entropy being a
thermodynamical function of state,
you understand."
At the other end of the phone I
nodded, not really getting it.
"You see," he continued, "as long as
the things in your room have energy,
they will always descend into chaos.
The only way to get rid of entropy is
to reduce the temperature to absolute
zero . . . two hundred and seventy-three
degrees below freezing."

I tried explaining the theory to Aunt Delle,
who hated anything scientific.
She pulled me out of Sunday school
right away and made me go into Big
Peoples Church, with all the adults. If
I was old enough to understand that
nonsense, she said, I was old enough
to lead prayers and do scripture
readings.

Meanwhile I started to leave my
bedroom windows open, even during the
winter. Of course there was no
chance of reducing the temperature
to absolute zero, but I thought that

lowering it might help.
It worked. Months later, the Bible
turned up at the bottom of the wash
basket.

Aunt Delle said that I was much
luckier than my brother because he
hardly ever saw Mum anymore and
she prayed that Levy would not turn
out like our Uncle Terry, who loved
money and white women too much
and that although he was a great
financial help, still needed to save his
soul.
In those days, Mum was getting very
thin but was still pretty. She wore
stonewash jeans and a tracksuit top
and her curly perm smelled like the
hairdressers. She would come over on
a Sunday every once in a while. Her and
Aunt Delle would shut the kitchen
door and talk. Then we would have
tea and Aunt Delle would get out the
fruitcake.
I loved those Sundays more than
anything. Mum didn't always come
when she said she would. But when
she did, they were my most favorite
days ever.
Mum eventually took up with

Washington, a rude, foul drunk with
body odor. He might really have
been quite attractive, only he
had no front teeth. That was why he
was known as Washington. He would
have been even more handsome than
Denzel with good dentistry and sober
habits.

Aunt Delle never liked my father but
she came to the funeral anyway,
wearing her best hat. I feel bad about
not seeing her enough. She still lives
alone, but she has home help. I don't
phone as often as I should. You
know how life is. We were round at
hers last night, Levy and I, staying
overnight before the funeral. I hadn't
been back there for a few years. We
ate snapper fish and dumplings off
the old willow-patterned crockery.
She didn't get the good Royal
Wedding plates out for us but she did
heat up some apple crumble in the
oven. Nothing much had changed in
the house apart from the old TV,
which had been replaced by some
newer model. It looked out of place
in the house, shiny and black and
new. She's getting very old. I know

the time will come when I'll phone
and she won't be there. So I try to
call out of duty every four weeks.

We are losing power.

Levy is pulling over towards the hard
shoulder. I am anxious. I want to get
back down south. The north is
unsettling, all deafening silences and
stressful boredom. There are not
nearly enough distractions and it can
all get too bloody silent, which leaves
room for dangerous things, like
thinking.

I ask Levy what is wrong with the car
and he says that there is nothing
wrong. He just doesn't feel right.
He has stopped on the hard shoulder
and I'm worried. I hope he isn't going
to have a heart attack or a
breakdown. A sane person doesn't go
around spitting in dead people's
coffins. So I ask if he feels breathless
or faint or anything.
He says,
"No, it is just a big feeling. One of
those crazy backed up against the wall
feelings, where every position hurts."

He says he's had them a lot lately.
Feelings like now there is no one left,
besides each other and Aunt Delle.
But she is old and she has Jesus. And
we've been too busy for Jesus lately.

"That big feeling you're talking
about," I say. "I think it's grief. Loss."
I tell him that it's just his mind's way
of coping, but really I have no idea
about his insides. If I did, I would be
able to work out why he only calls
twice a year.
He coughs and asks me if I've cried
since I heard the news. I tell him I
haven't cried about anything since
Mum died. I feel slightly
uncomfortable that my big brother is
getting so deep, to tell you the truth.
It would be too strange for him to
start now.
Levy says sorry for leaving. I know he
is talking about just now, about
leaving me alone in the church like
that, but I wish that he were talking
about when I was six and lost him.
He mumbles something about having
to get back to London and looks like
he is going to start up the ignition
again which is a good idea because it's
dangerous and illegal, isn't it, to be
parked up here like this?

He looks older than thirty.
I know it is going to be some time
before I speak to him again
and I know it shouldn't be like this
but it is what it is.
God, we really should get going. Here
we are, both busy people, still sitting
here in the car on the hard shoulder.
Staring out of the front window,
not crying our eyes out.

panacea

You told me I seemed haunted.
It was three a.m. and you could still smell
the storm clouds under my skin.
You can't quell depression by making
love.
But we tried.
But we tried,
oh, we did.

mental health

If you're walking down an aisle with a
dim, fluorescent hue
by the tinned fish and canned beans
strip lighting above, cracked tiles
beneath
with the realization that most things
are futile
and get the sudden urge to end it all
don't stop. Call a friend.
Call your mother if you have one
and, if you can stand her,
listen to her talk about the price of
canned fish and tinned beans.
Call the speaking clock. Know that
whatever time it says is the time that
everything has to change.
Leave the damn aisle.
Don't go anywhere where they sell
sweets, chips, booze,
fast love or lottery tickets.

See that just outside there are people-
lined streets that are emptier than
your insides,
skies darker than your own.
Look for yourself, because it never
helps to hear from anyone else.

If you are one of those "running
around town like mad" people,
people who jump from tall buildings,
buildings with glass fronts and not enough
air
if you are failing to fix a broken story
if you have been cooped up for far
too long in a very high tower in a
dangerously low state
plenty of TV channels and TV
dinners. Plenty of biscuits, chocolate
desserts, cake and plenty of wine but
no love for miles and miles

if you did not get up for work today
if it has been afternoon for hours
and the silence is keeping you awake,
if you only remember how to draw
your breath in and out like waves of
thick tar cooling,
if you are wishing it later,
pulling the sun down with your
prayers, leave the damn bed.
Wash the damn walls. Crack open a
window
even in the rain. Even in the snow.

Listen to the church bells outside.
Know that however many times they
chime is half the number of changes
you have to make.

Stop trying to die. Serve your time
here.
Do your time.

Clean out the fridge.
Throw away the soya milk. Soya milk
is made from children's tears. Put
flowers on the table. Stand them in a
measuring jug. Chop raw vegetables if
you have them.
Know that if you are hungry for
something but you can't think what
you are, more often than not, only
love-thirsty
only bored.

When the blood in your body is
weary to flow,
when your bones are heavy though
hollow
if you have made it past thirty
celebrate
and if you haven't yet,
rejoice. Know that there is a time
coming in your life when dirt settles
and the patterns form a picture.

If you dream of the city but you live
in the country
milk the damn cows.
Sell the damn sheep.

Know that they will be wishing you
well
posing for pictures on milk cartons or
running over lush hills to be counted
at the beginning of somebody else's
dream.
See, they never held you back.
It was you, only you.

nose

In all theories,
I have written you out of my memory.
Still, the middle of my face
refuses to be told.

I'm undone. Perhaps it is the breeze in my head.
Three years. And I did too much work on our love.
Three years
and I can't undo the problem of your scent.

It is a horrid and complicated fact. My fifth sense
an ambush. I walk by a bakery, chip shop, flower
stall, shopping center,
leather goods store

all the mornings in Lancashire still smell like you.
Last week I was caught in a storm overseas. When
the rain smell drove me silly
all I could feel were your hands.

Now home, I light the stove. I cook new food these
days
from recipe books. Now that you're gone I can fry
meat.
I buy a perfume I know you hate
and spray it on your side of the bed.

Still
you greet me in waves I cannot decipher.
Last night I smelled you in a dream. It is a
thumbprint now but I can't forget the loss.

I dreamed you beautiful.
You are
nothing beautiful. But
three years
and I can't clean you off my skin.

issue

I have searched hard for my very
dead parents in women with my
father's stature and men with my
mother's features
almost unwittingly
hardly successfully.

I like the sounds
our bodies make
when they fall in like.

I love the word *love*,
I do
but only far from home.

what is now will soon be past

Just because you do it
doesn't mean you always will.
Whether you're dancing dust
or breathing light
you're never exactly the same,
twice.

why you love her and what to do

I

Because she, like you, was raised on the
hard side of the lie and when this giant
of a woman folds all of herself into you
so small, you want to keep her for good
—safe from all that ever was and will be.
You want to take her away from
everything that ever hurt her or still can

because neither of you know your
daddy's voice.
You know first name and surname and
little facts like the country hers was born
in and that yours had puppy dog eyes
that cut through your mother's
stubbornness
but as for his shade of black and the way
your hands might feel in his . . . you may
only guess

because you joke that perhaps they were
the same person . . . that would explain so
much and would also make you illegal,
but some of the best loves have been

because you knew her past before she
told you—those were all of your
mistakes too, happening in a different
town aged sixteen with grown men
some of whom had grown wives

because your bodies always betrayed
your young selves—making you smell
like you shouldn't, giving you a scent
you weren't yet old enough to own
doing women's work when you were
barely old enough to bear a man's
weight, a heartbreak, or a child. This is
why you love her.

II

So you've got to hold her with both
hands at arm's length.
Say there's too much of her inside of
you already. Feel like you cannot stand
any more. Tell her no, pull back, it
hurts.
Know that she scares you and you're
far too used to life as a lone wolf crying
at the new moon and marveling at its
orientation in every single new country.
Let her know the relief of leaving things
behind. Tell her it's a pain you've
grown with. Tell her you'll come back.
Visit. Really mean it.

Tell her she is better with someone else.
The kind of person who stays in a place
and builds and knows how to stay put.
Know that her mothering isn't
something to get used to. Tell her you
stopped relying on this aged six.
See her happy in the future with
someone better than you. Feel sick
when you feel it, but know it.

q

If you
were married to yourself
could you stay with yourself?

My house
would be frightening and wild.

another tuesday

I bet
there are millions of stories
in your legs alone

a man tells a girl
while he is pulling on his boxers and
gray socks.
I love my wife,
he says,
putting on his trousers.
I just need the fire,
he says shivering.
Your kind of fire.

It is December.
She nods and thinks
that he looks like something else,
standing there
glistening, self-important
about to drive two miles home to his family.

She has a bedsit
and a healthy dream life
long brown legs and the kind of eyes that
sink you.
Too much sadness in her
but so much youth
it doesn't quite show, not yet.

Odd how
often
beauty is another type of prison.

But what can you do?
He pays one full hundred
and really when you need it, you need it.
She did well at school
but large thoughts are a problem
when there's no call for them.
They become a nuisance,
always reminding you of the ghost life
running alongside you,

the phantom life
you could have had
if you felt at home
if everyone where you grew up
didn't get off their heads.
If there's nothing like the next high
if you cook magic in your kitchen
who needs food
when it takes you and sends you on to Venus,
it doesn't matter when you get
chest pains
or sick
or forget how to speak
if your veins are driving you out to sea.

So she offers up her arms
gets lost in the pretty side of life
in the crevices

slips into its hot folds
when Tuesday rolls into Thursday
and there's no night anymore

no night
just ink-blue blankets
dusted with hours of star
warm
engulfed
gilt-edged minutes.

In a place
where nothing stings.
Not a thing.

success

"I'm two hundred percent of a lover
and it gets me into trouble,"

you laugh
fooling no one
not even yourself

yes, you're a beauty. Yes
people want you
but only at first.

Your talents just about ruin your life.

Yes. You are dazzling
yes
you'll make money
but only too much
and fast.

Yes. You'll be rich
but only in cash.

the biggest tortoise in the world

"They found the biggest tortoise
in the world in South America today,"
you said, massaging the tender knot at the back of
my neck
with one hand
removing your boots
with the other.
"They had to get a lorry or something to remove
it, imagine that."
I said nothing, thinking of all of the things you
understand and
all of the things you don't
like how I will love you forever but
probably from afar
not in the way you want and
how you'll find somebody new
to be with. It's only fair.
Maybe he or she will have
tightness in the neck
a passion for useless facts
the power to stick around and
really, I miss you already.

now that it's all over

She says she cries over me on the
train to and from work
and one day it will be better but it
isn't better now.
she is just like my mother, but alive.
Knows how to love
quietly, completely.
Something about the way black women
hold your heart.

You can leave them all you like but you
can't stay gone.

what love isn't

It is not a five-star stay. It is not
compliments and it is never ever
flattery.
It is solid. Not sweet but always
nutritious
always herb, always salt. Sometimes
grit.
It is now and till the end. It is never a
slither, never a little
it is a full serving
it is much
too much and real
never pretty or clean. It stinks—you can
smell it coming
it is weight
it is weight and it is too heavy to feel
good sometimes. It is discomfort—it is
not what the films say. Only songs
get it right
it is irregular
it is difficult
and always, always
surprising.

body

If I'm entirely honest,
and you say I must be,
I want to stay with you all afternoon
evening, night and tomorrow
pressed into you so tightly that we don't
know whose belly made what sound,
whose heart it is that is thumping like
that
until I don't know if the sweat on my
chest is yours or mine or ours.

**things it can take twenty years
and a bad liver to work out**

1.

Truth is a beauty, whether pretty or not.

Love doesn't always mean you should stay.

Sometimes the truth has to punch you, twice.

Love doesn't always mean you should stay.

2.

See, nobody warns you about yourself.
The red in your eye.
The trap in your mouth.

The person who hurts you the most in the end will
be you.
Almost every time, you.

You'd better learn to forgive yourself.
Forgive yourself instantly.
It's a skill you're going to need until you die.

3.

When the girl is all kinds of weather in a day
do not enter her lightly.
Your senses will not survive it.
You can leave your tail,
head, eye lights on
come, go hollow
running away from her
without any of the good parts of yourself
thinking you did nothing wrong.

Wondering why,
when you smile,

blood.

4.

Love is not a safe word.

But it's the safe things that kill you
in the end.

5.

You lose too much to fear.
You might choke on all that you do not say

and

can we talk about when it should be no
but you say yes?

6.

There are parts of you
that want the sadness.
Find them out. Ask them why.

7.

Make it.
If you don't
it will be a tragedy

and then

everything else

the sky
and everything else.

lipsing

Some lovers look you in the mouth
right clean in your mouth
and your story comes,
running.

revelation

One day I will tell you what I've been.
It will scare you.

sabbath

Your skirt is split too high for church.
The elders glare.
You are your mother's daughter.
Always meaning well and falling short.
Where is she these days?
they inquire
with knowing faces.

You don't give them anything.
You say,
Paris this week, then on to Italy.

They say, *oh that's nice*
with their mouths
and the air says all the rest.

You don't care.
Everyone says you have her face and it's a face
that'll open doors.
Even locked doors. Especially locked doors

and so,

the skirt is split too high for church
but the collection box is yours.
You look like an actress,
says the usher.
Sit here. Right here. Relax.

not the end of the world, but almost

The day was not the best, especially in
my head. I was thinking calmly
about stepping off the side of the
mountain in the rain
arms outstretched
embracing this life, this empty space
one last time and making it look like
an accident. My eyes were blurry with
salt and I hadn't eaten in days but my
mind was clearer than air on a blue-
sky morning in the Black Country.

I said,

No hard feelings bright, hard world
but maybe
just maybe you are not for me. Maybe
I'm stretched too thinly, pressed too
deeply into you in a shape that I can't
keep without cramping and maybe
just maybe your breath is too cold.
Perhaps human nature is just too
fickle to understand
and rainbows aren't all they're cracked
up to be, so why hang on until the
rain ends?

That was when I saw you.
Eyes did meet, lightning did not
flash but I thought to myself, Who
wears a reindeer jersey and red shorts
in May? And anyway you looked kind
and the sun was peeping out a little
and the sky was still dark and it was
still drizzling but everyone needs a
little kindness.

You have a smile that turns down at
the corners
and those gentle kind of eyes.

Those gentle kind of eyes.

We sat on a hill in the car looking at
where the beach met the sea and the
rain hit them both and I (quite
desperately, quite selfishly) said, Drive
into the sea with me, just once and
it's done.
You drove fast in the opposite
direction to a blessed place of broken
brick and stone and said, This used to
be my childhood house, and then
drove me further
on further
to a purple house safe up on the
hillside and said, Hey,
one day this will be home.

It wasn't perfect. It isn't now. I still
have days when I want to exit the
system quicker than you can say don't
you dare give up now
and you still have days where you
can't even taste the sweet in raw
honey and neither one of us believes
in pills.
Days when I so want to kiss you but
your mouth is sour and my thoughts
are bitter and I'm angry, just mad, just
crazy with it all
but we are each other's home sweet
home, Love.
The roof is screwed on too tight at
times and the walls of our house can
pinch a little but, my God, they are
always warm.

waiting for the check to clear

What an odd, romantic time it is, if
you remember not to panic.
How many times has money almost
driven you mad?
You only need spices to throw in the
bowl
you only need flour to make some
kind of bread
and maybe somebody to lie in the
dark with.
Somebody's hands to touch.

a

Your father died this morning.
I scramble to the supermarket to buy a
phone card and call South Africa
from the bottom deck of a South
London bus.

You sound smaller than you are.
"I am wearing a skirt," you say, "can
you imagine?"
I cannot. All I can think is in your
language
oh God, Ngiyakuthanda.
My God,
how you are loved.

You cannot speak for long
you have family to sit with
sweet tea to steep,
a mother to attend to
food in plastic and foil to warm
and stow away

"Okay," I say, reaching the stop
by Camberwell. "Let me know when
I can call."
I hang up.

The sky
is trying to rain and all I can speak
is in your language
into the broken line
into the dead space.
Oh God.
Ngiyakukhumbula.
My God,
how you are missed.

some kind of man

He kept trying to explain. When he
tried the first time, she didn't get it.
When he explained again, she didn't
want to understand. The more that he
tried to tell her, the less she wanted to
know. He smelled of something
strong and sweet. Perfume. Not
liquor.

"Believe me," Samuel had begged,
and as soon as he said that she felt as
though she never would again. "It's
not what you think." He was right about
that. It was far beyond
anything that she could ever have
imagined. She felt as though she
would die. The worst thing about
somebody who betrays you,
somebody who turns out to be a
completely different person to whom
you first thought, is the love that you
still feel in your heart for them,
embedded so deeply into the narrow
spaces of yourself that you cannot
access it to try and remove it.

He said, "I'm so sorry. I'm so, so sorry. This doesn't mean what you think."

She slapped him in the face and the more he stood there and took it and the more she collapsed into tears, the more she loved him and could not understand it.

But everybody knew what kind of man he was. He was the kind of man who, when you woke up in the middle of the night itching on the joints of your fingers and your legs and jaw line because the mosquitoes had been at you again, would rub cold ointment into your skin whispering, "Hush baby, you will be fine." Or if you felt like you were going to be sick and cried because you were scared of vomiting, held your body with one hand and stroked your hair with the other, who checked your fever when you said you had a temperature, who would cut the crust off your sandwiches and pick all of the apricot pieces that you didn't like out of your muesli in the morning. It had all been too good to be true and his behaving exactly like a

saint at all times had only served to
set her up for the fall.

Perhaps she should have known.
Indeed, she should have known. She
wanted to blame his mother. His
sisters. Somebody. She decided that
these things—the devil's work—strike
as a kind of test. She would have to
deal with it immediately.

It was evening on the sixth day.
According to the calendar, the sunset
was in forty-five minutes and there
were far too many things to do
before then. She wanted to write
something about it all on the lines
provided under this week's Bible
study notes. A prayer. Something
about masculinity. Something about
loss. But it was all too fresh. She
hadn't ever seen him cry before that
evening. He told her that he was
sorry, again and again. Kept telling
her that she was all that he needed.

There were things to be done.
By nightfall that evening she was on
her knees praying because the
Sabbath was upon them. The lunch

boxes had been packed for church
and their boy was in bed, dreaming
about Jesus and spaceships.
What did this mean for her now?
What would they do next? Was it safe
to have the father continue living
there? She felt guilty at the thought.

Right after it happened, Samuel took
the car. Didn't know quite where he
was going. Drove awhile. Drank
some soup by the roadside. Decided
that the only place to go right now
was Benny's.
He didn't dare consider what he
might have lost. Each time he tried to
process what had happened, his
breathing became light and his
temples thudded until they were sore.

Benny didn't say anything when he
came to the door. He stepped aside
to let Samuel in and didn't speak,
except to ask him if he needed to
breathe into a paper bag and if he
wanted some Scotch. Samuel declined
the drink but took the bag. Benny left
him sitting on the bed in the back
room, staring hard at the mirror on
the wall.

A short while later Samuel could
hear Benny moving about in the
kitchen, whistling and sweeping up
the porch. He was tired. He heard the
television. He wondered if he should
fast and pray on this. But he already felt
weak of heart and spirit. His
vision was blurred. He wondered
what it was that he needed to do
from now to make everything right
again. But had it been right before?

Benny was looking at the television,
but he wasn't watching it. He was
thinking about the situation regarding
the man in the back room, namely the
man's wife and the little boy.
Wondering what would happen. If
she would talk. That said, he didn't
know how much Samuel had told
her. He was wondering why this type of
thing had to be such a big deal. If he were
braver and didn't value his
own privacy so much—if he was
younger, angrier, he might have been
an activist. Self-expression is a tricky
thing. Just as you start to feel
comfortable with yourself after years
of not, you then have to justify
yourself to other people.

He was sure that Samuel would come out of the room when he was ready. He continued squinting at the TV, peering at the shapes and people moving around, staring at the corners of the set and the metal and the digital lines, began to dream.

He had always known what he wanted to do, but had waited patiently until his father died. His father would have called it evil. Most people still did but generally those he helped would keep private things private. He wondered what Samuel had said. Hoped that his wife wasn't going to take it to those crazy people in the church tomorrow, because he believed those people to be the most dangerous. His father had been a long-standing member at the church and had raised the children there. He sucked in a lungful and exhaled, the smoke rings unfurling in the air.

It had all started with shoes. As a young boy, he had developed a wonderful fascination with the curve of a woman's foot in a shoe. He drew them on paper over and

over again. A heel. A boot. Benny
had always loved to make clothes for
his sister's dolls and could not
understand why everyone was so
horrified. He had grown up with
three brothers, two sisters and his
blind father, who beat the hell out of
him when he announced that he
wanted to make women's clothing.
Never mind the fact that most of the
famous designers up in Europe and
America were all men. His father told
him that he wasn't raising that kind of
boy and that he would learn to do
something else with his life.
Nobody argued with his father, ever.

Benny started creating aged thirty, the
same day they buried his father. He
took a lover for the first time too, a
twenty-three-year-old from the next
parish, who assured him that he could
make a business out of his gift. He took
the advice and between
dancehall wear and alternative outfits,
began to be known in the area for his
costumes and undergarments.
Known to those who knew. Some
men would go to him to buy outfits
for their wives, in larger sizes than he
knew their wives to be.

Samuel was lying down in the back room. If he were home now he would be polishing Michael's little black shoes on the blue tile steps to the doorway, the warm aroma of peanut porridge wafting from the kitchen. He wanted to go home and sort out the mess he'd made. Beg for her forgiveness and put all of this behind him. He had slipped. He usually kept apparel hidden at Benny's and one moment of carelessness had caused all of this. He opened the right-hand door of the wardrobe and took out a shoe. A court shoe. A delicate, high-heeled court shoe. Elegant, even in his size. A blue satin court shoe with a silver insole. It was so beautifully done. He cradled it against his chest, thought of Tessa and fell asleep.

In the little house, Tessa was listening to a gospel CD and trying to study the Bible. Trying to speak to God. She was trying to do everything at once. Each time she thought about what happened earlier she wanted to throw up.

She called him over when she saw the plastic bag containing the underwear stuffed underneath a roll of bin liners in the boot of the car. A black bustier with gold embellishments on it and French panties. Not her size.

She had been angry and hurt at the thought of another woman but in the end she would have handled it fine. Another woman she would have been able to take. She had married him fully prepared for it. Supposed that with this beautiful man a whole foot taller than her with smooth dark skin, a square jaw and high cheekbones, it would only be a matter of time. In town, women stared at him all the time.
People had always considered him too attractive. Said she was looking for trouble with a man so handsome.

So when she heard the ludicrous explanation she couldn't believe it. Maybe it was someone at church. Yes, maybe that was it. But he had never lied to her about anything before. And that pain in his face, that shame. When he had stared at her and said, "They are mine," she wanted to laugh. But one look at her husband and she had known that it was true.

She wondered if they just couldn't put it all behind them. Perhaps with prayer and help from the church as a collective. Her stomach churned again as she imagined him dressed up as *somebody's woman*. How dare he. How dare he ruin what they had spent years building, with a beautiful little boy and good jobs, both of them. How could he? Couldn't he put away this perversion when his family was at risk?

Samuel woke up with an ache between his ribs and saw that it was the shoe heel. He could hear Benny snoring from the living room. On his knees he began to pray for any sign. He wondered if he should leave the country. Follow his sister to Miami and send the child money from over there. What kind of role model was he, anyway? What kind of man was he? He was a man who was in love

with his wife, loved his son and
wanted to be who he was. He wanted
all of those to coexist. Was that
wrong?

In the morning, Tessa got up and
prepared herself for church. She got
Michael dressed and ready. There was
no car to take them to church so they
walked.
The two of them arrived there after
the early morning Bible school. The
bottom of Michael's trousers were
dusty and they were both sweating a
little. She took her place on a pew,
and ushered Michael towards the
front to sit with the other children.
She heard one of the ladies behind
her whisper that they wouldn't let
their son leave the house with such
dirty shoes. The other lady whispered
that the little boy's hair was looking
rough and should have been combed
out better. Tessa's face burned and
she stared straight ahead, putting a
hand to her own hair, which was
shining and pressed into obedience.
She wished that she had combed her
child's hair better and that her
husband didn't like to dress in

women's clothes. She wished that she wasn't going to lose everything.

Perhaps he was not mentally sound. He had never been like other men, wanting to run around and father children all over the place. He never looked at other women.

Indeed, she should have known. He was God-fearing and quiet and always ready to help. Had she been inadequate as a woman maybe? Perhaps she had let him help around the house too much? She had been unwell for a while. Yes, her head had become quite sick after she gave birth to Michael and hardly wanted to look at the child. Samuel was left with the baby, having to play the mother's role. Perhaps it was that. She shivered in the house of the Lord and begged forgiveness. Most days she still looked at the child and although she wanted to care for him so much, she didn't feel what she imagined she should. But that was between her and her God, not her and the child.

A lady in church was giving a testimony about how she became a Christian, how she had put away her

friends who had vices, how she
preferred to live alone rather than
around improper influences.
Tessa decided to take this to the
church. She felt moved to speak
freely among her brothers and sisters
in Christ.

When she rose to her feet to speak, a
respectful quiet ran through the
church. Her voice rang pure and clear
as she called on the Father, the Son and
the Holy Spirit, asking for help from the
Trinity and the heavenly
angels surrounding them. She told
them. Asked for their guidance,
comfort and support. There was a
silence. Somebody offered to anoint
her. She felt hands on her, from her
head to her shoulders, waist and legs.
She was vibrating, *pulsing* with the
energy of the church family. It was
quite unlike anything that she had felt
before. Everybody was murmuring
and praying and holding hands. Some
ladies were speaking in tongues. One
of them fainted and one was violently
sick but nobody was perturbed
because it was all down to the will of
the spirit.

No soul was left unmoved in the church building that morning. This *epidemic,* they all decided, was cause for grave concern. The brother in need had to be saved. It was the church's responsibility as a unit, a *body.* They couldn't allow another soul to be destroyed. They needed to talk, needed to pray, needed to get rid of those demons that were around infecting everybody's children and some people's husbands and ruining the country economically, spiritually and politically. It just wasn't right.

Three p.m., said the pastor. Let us reconvene. Let us meet in the street, march to him and save him. Please be godly in the respect that three p.m. means three p.m. No black people's time please. Some people found this funny, but the pastor had been serious.

By four thirty p.m. Benny could make out the gathering of church people in the distance. They were singing choruses and praying for a successful outcome. The dust on the ground was red and the skyline was tinted orange. They were marching towards the house, singing hymns. Miss Phillips was leading in song with her haunting melodic voice and the male voice choir behind her, backing her up. Everyone was wearing white. They marched deliberately, synchronized at a slow, slow pace with a nod of the head on each step. As they drew nearer, Tessa was calling out for her husband.

Samuel appeared on the porch behind Benny. She glimpsed the husband who she was there to save and saw that he was beautiful. There were people in the neighborhood gathering around mass on Benny's front yard. The pastor had begun to preach, *"Repent, dear sons. Repent!"* and there was a ripple of assent in the crowd and shouts of "Only repenting will save you, sons." Onlookers were joining, pushing in and jostling to see what was going on. Children were running, trying to keep up with the church musicians. Skipping around the congregation to see what all of the excitement was about. And there was dancing. No hips gyrating, of course. No bottom shaking, naturally. Waving and clapping, hands and faces pointing heavenward to Jesus as the hymns got louder and the churchgoers excited.

Some people from the area whom she felt sure did not go to church were arriving with fire and kerosene. The churchgoers were singing about being soldiers. They were singing,

"We are soldiers
in God's army.
We're going to fight,
and some will have to die."

They were singing about holding up a blood-stained banner and then a fire arose from the back room of the house. Not turning around, Benny's heart shot out to all the corners of his body as he felt his life, fabric and memories burning.

Unruffled and more concerned with the task in hand, the churchgoers sang on. These sinners needed to be saved and a few flames were a small price to pay. After all, there would be more fire in the pits of hell.

The pastor continued and the crowd
moved closer towards them. Tessa
was soon pushed out of the way by
others who had joined the gathering.

And on second glance, some of those
who appeared to be dancing were
shaking fists and some who appeared to
be singing were hurling abuse at
the two men. This she hadn't
prepared for. The rage. The
revulsion. Shouts of that word, that
awful word. This was all wrong.
Wrong and surely not what the
church had intended at all. It had
become dangerous. Disturbing.
People were preventing their children
from running into harm's way.
The police arrived on the scene with their
beef patties and grape sodas in
enough time to get a good view of
proceedings, smiles on their round
faces.

The two men did not run. The smoke
rose, thick and black.

true story

It's not that Dad doesn't love you
or your brother,
said Mum,
greasing up our ashy legs with Vaseline
Or that your Auntie Amy's a man-
stealing, cheating, back-stabbing bitch
who can't keep a man so she has to steal
somebody else's.
We just don't see eye to eye anymore,
that's all
and he wouldn't stop eating cashew
nuts in bed.

It's not that your mum and I
hate each other,
said Dad, pushing a crumpled ten
pound note into my chinos pocket
or that I forgot about your birthday
but I need time to think. I'm moving
in with Amy
and anyway, your mum cooks with
too much salt.

It wasn't so much an affair, you
understand,
said Auntie Amy, lacing up my

brother's small Nike trainers
and picking out my knots with the
wooden comb shaped like a fist
but a meeting of minds,
outside of our respective vows.
(And bodies, muttered Mum when
I told her later.
Two-faced tramp. What a joke.
Don't tell anyone I said that.
Don't tell anyone I said that.)

It's not as though
your mum's exactly an angel, either,
said Dad with bloodred eyes
and a pulsing vein in his forehead
finishing the last of the whisky
and Auntie Amy said, Easy Winston,
you've had a lot
and Dad said, Don't tell me what to
do
not even my wife yet, and you think
you know it all.
Yeah, you think you know it all?

It's not that your family are going to
hell, necessarily,
said Grandma, boiling up the green
banana, yam and dumpling
and grating the coconut onto the rice
and peas.

They must just accept Jesus Christ
into their lives
and put away the drink and sin and all
the lies.
Now go and wash your hands and set
the table.
Don't worry, girl.
We'll pray for them tonight.

breathe

If in the end her words were nothing
if in the end his hands were air
if the thought of her rips.
If he stopped phoning when you stopped
fucking
if she hangs on you
and
doesn't call again
if he asks you to pay back the money.
If.

If she still isn't sorry
if.

karma

The
girl who made your life hell
when you were young and had no friends
walked by you today. Names are not important
here
but feelings are

because sometimes
you find yourself, some twenty years later
or more
still cowering
still minuscule speaking
still tiny lettering
all the way in your stomach. Still
a swallower of things.

You always thought karma would get her
but you hear she's doing well. Got married,
kids on the way, not that you're really definitely
after those
things
but
still.
Still
it's a bitch.

You came home
many times feeling
ghoul. All kinds of transparent.
Do the feelings ever
leave? Or do you just learn to wrap them up into
something to wear?
That's one thing everything does, you suppose.
Turns you into a maker of gold.

14

But at least I'm not fourteen
anymore,
talking to other people's husbands
avoiding my stepfather
drinking all of the clear stuff I can
find in my
mother's cabinet,
washing it down with talcum powder
and orange juice
passing out in parks
or at football games
and getting the dark, dark chills
in the early hours of the morning.
Staying forever far from home
completely, completely at sea.
Knowing God has cut me out
jagged, loose, wild.

prayer

Some girls do
and I'm one of them.
They told me God didn't like it.

I cried at church
tried to pray myself Good.
(Sat on my hands.)

Some girls do
and I'm one of them.

They told me *men* wouldn't like it.
I plaited my hair
tried to quiet the singing down there
(I was sitting on hymns.)

Some girls do
and I'm one of them.

They said I really didn't like it
(not if I was honest with myself).

I sat at the meetings
(confessed to things
that have never felt wrong)

things that some girls do
and
I tell you,
I'm one of them.

Hungry. Stomach screaming hungry, I worry about the conversation we haven't had yet. You know, this one. I will order pudding after dinner and chew and swallow without tasting anything much. You will chain-smoke and drink three different beers and we will talk out how to make the best of things despite the year and its shitty weather. We are tired of dressing in layers just in case and leaving wet umbrellas in other people's houses. Who can live like that? On the day, your voice will be too bright and cheerful, the way it always is when you hurt the most. We're always trying to make everything *okay. Fine. Well,* or whatever shit we tell our friends instead of awful. Grieving. Barely breathing. Come, let us talk with our closed-up throats, crushed hearts and wet eyes. Quickly, because when you get that metallic taste on your tongue and teeth it means trouble and when I get that light feeling in the space between the back of my eyes and my skull it means hell.

the stupid thing about it

You're on the phone for four whole hours. While your head hurts and you can't go on and you wish you'd never met. While she blames you and you blame her and she hates you and you hate her
still, in the end, it goes like this

You: I need to touch you. I want you.
Her: Come over, right now. Hurry.

new

hold me, you.
firmly, because all I've known how to
do so far is leave

hold me, you.
tightly, because all I've known how to
do so far is run

challenge me, because all I've known
so far is how to make excuses.

The other day I told you your mind
was a different country
you said, "No. Continent," and we
laughed.

When I joke about having other
lovers you tell me they're all in you so
where would I be running to?

You are a million different reasons to
stop. I don't sleep as much as I
thought I needed to
or drink all the wine. I'm frightened I
might be happy.
Dig your nails in.
All I've known how to do so far is
walk.

quirk

You are one of life's
anomalies
and this is
how I fell.

up home

Stuff that you remind me of.
Home. Wherever that is. I'm
confused

and in the same way that my grandma
(who hasn't seen my brother or me for
two years because he has been lost
somewhere between despair and
north Manchester
and I've been away in Africa)

in the same way that she just smiles
and puts on the kettle
I'm beginning to feel a lot like I'll
wait for you
against my better judgment.

She gives us macaroni and brown
stew chicken in a Tupperware box
(which she asks him to return but
everyone knows he won't).
Core loneliness is a terrible thing.
I suppose we all have each other, but
only up to a certain point.
I suppose we all die stubbornly and
separately, in the end.

Someone reads Psalms 139
and, in the verse that mentions how
we are fearfully and wonderfully
made,
I'm beginning to see the light
and I trace the outlines of your
tattoos on my arm.

My brother takes all of the food
because he had mouths to feed.
Nobody knows how many. Nobody
has asked or kept count and he
doesn't say much. Anyway, I will soon
be en route to London. Can't
have food and memories weighing
me down, however delicious.

Some things you just have to leave up
North, like short a's, Morrisons,
Ovaltine, pictures of your late parents
in graduation caps and gowns

carrot juice the way West Indian
people make it with the nutmeg and
condensed milk
and the look on your grandparents'
faces, always, when you say,

"Oh well, must get going. Don't want
to miss my train."

I'm beginning to miss you terribly, by
the way.
It's a stunning day up here
despite the rain.

mum

Mum. Where you are
I hope that there is Tia Maria and
Coca-Cola
and people don't talk too loudly when
you're trying to sleep.
I hope you have a daughter with a
plan and a dream
and sons who aren't on first-name
terms with the police.
I hope you have your pick of a few
good men
and none of them know how to
cheat.

Mum, where you are . . . I hope that
there are grandfathers who don't
stare at you for too long
and grandmas who aren't sick
I hope that they don't scream because
your mother left
and tell you,
you ain't shit.
I hope that you don't bathe old men
for a living
who call you nigger bitch

Mum, where you are, I hope that God
comes down and shows you what
goes where
and doesn't shout because you're far
too tired to care.

I hope that there's someone to tease
the knots out of your hair.
I hope that good is good and right is
right and fair is fair.

kid

You can fit two thousand four
hundred and ninety-six
tiny letter a's on an a4 page
based on fitting four of them firmly
into the space of a
centimeter square.
Dad will say, "That's diligence for
you."
Everyone else will call it a waste of
time.

You can fit a whole tube of Smarties
in your mouth
while dressing your little brother up
in your Sunday best.
Grandma will laugh at the boy in the
dress.
Granddad will nearly hit someone.
Your brother will be sent upstairs to
change
head bowed in shame.
No one will notice the Smarties.

Mum says fifty-six bad words on the
phone to Jamaica.
She is not impressed when you tell
her so.

"Keep out of adult conversations,"
she warns,
her mouth growing tight.
The pastor makes twenty-four
references to hell
in the sermon at church and forgets
to talk
about love. Granddad falls asleep.

If your Bible has pictures
you should color them in and count
how many men in the church wear
white socks and black shoes.
Count the bitten fingernails and
how many people cry silently during
prayer.

Count the number of cars that
afternoon before your mother,
tired and lovely, pulls up on the
pavement to collect you.
Count how many people shake their
head at her red nails, her tight jeans.
She looks like a star and they're
jealous.

You can fit the word *lonely*
four hundred and sixteen times
on the back of that same piece of
paper.
Dad will say, "Don't be silly. Your

brother will be out of hospital soon."
Mum will be too stressed to talk.
You will go to live at Grandma's,
spending days drinking rooibos out
of egg cups,
studying God's word and watching
the sun.

You will learn to fear
The *Most High*
also
count how many times the
King James Bible uses the words *thee,
thou* and *thy.*
Keep a proper tally. Granddad can
play any song on the harmonica.
Test him. He likes to be tested
(until he doesn't know the answer.
Then he will get angry
and say things he doesn't mean).

There are one hundred and twenty-
seven roses
on the wallpaper in your new room.
There were more than that but you
picked some away.
Your brother has been gone now for
two months straight and
nobody will tell you anything.
Count how many
family friends are praying for you.

There are sixty-four red grapes on
the bunch
eat one after the other, fast
without stopping.
Maybe you can visit the hospital too.

inconvenience

I'll never understand you,
but my God,
how I want you.

You happen very suddenly
before I have time to do what I usually do
to stay safe.

I try it all, to find you arrogant, dull,
unkind. Nothing works
and I dream you up
like a fiend.

You flick your eyes over me
and it goes straight to my
fourth brain. Even your
breathing excites me.

And we all know
the dangers that lie ahead. My cells make room
for you.

My breathing is light
My head is filled silly
My reason darkens.

coordinates

Every time I travel
I meet myself a little more.
Sometimes you have to leave all your cities
to fall in love

and now I am
time zones apart from
most of my lovers,
some lives apart from the others.

who was doing what and where

She was in the kitchen. Not crying.
Not crying, I said.
He was in the hallway
already gone,
like the rest of them.
We were in the living room. Not
caring. Not caring, mind you.
Perhaps we did. Perhaps we cared
(a bit).
Perhaps she did a bit of crying too.

on hearing he hit his girlfriend

Your brother shuffles in his seat
looking uncomfortable when you say,
"What if someone were to do that to
me," and mumbles, "I'd fuck them
up. You know I'd fuck them up."
He cannot look you in the eye today.
It's the one time in twentysomething
years that you don't instinctively feel
the need to make him feel better
about himself
or lament the plight of mixed-up
black boys from broken homes
or consider the flawed system
it's the one time in twentysomething
years
that he's more the culprit
much less the victim
so you clear your throat
(purposefully)
and say,
"That's inexcusable and one corner I
won't stand in to fight for you
so you'd better talk. Now."
So you sit down to talk
and he cries, mostly.

when they ask

W hen they ask you how you are
don't say fearful. Narrow your eyes
and kiss your teeth but don't say
afraid.

Don't say more scared than
ever before, or floundering.
Don't say lost without
cause or that you're not always sure
you can make it.
Straighten that back
you are sex. Look like sex.

Wipe the blood from yourself.
Don't tell them what went on when
the sun was busy in another street.

Do that Thing The People Do.
The people who are fine, fine, fine
until you get home and find them
gone, gone, gone.

Keep suffering because it's your God-
Given Right.
Brawl with your being. Fight the bad
fight.

Fight.

If they ask you how you are
don't say stolen. Don't say forgotten,
passed over,
ignored. Don't you dare say Orphan.
Don't say beaten by the system
oppressed and disturbed
and don't you dare say disappointed
don't you dare say damaged.

Smile.
Smile with all of your teeth, even the
rotting ones.
Even the rotting ones.

to the elders

I cannot find the God you serve
and I have been known to stay out all
night, searching.

history

1.

A new man kissed me
when I was sixteen
and
not on the mouth
either.
Now granted, he was looking after me
and I was too old
for my own good.

And granted he had a wife
and I had a mother
an awful stepdad and a little brother
and granted
I wanted to die
most days.

Granted he didn't take my
virginity
—that was long gone
but something of a different kind
left me.

no.
left me
I don't think so

left me
I don't feel good when . . .
left me
or
honestly
they were never mine.

2.

The man who kissed me
wanted to leave his wife
and right away, too.
Now, granted he was moving too fast
and I wanted out.
And granted he liked a drink
and by then so did I.

I left though, in the end.
Two cases of beer and a thirst for something else.

I'm still looking for
the words to get me out
of these things.

untitled 1

If you're afraid to write it,
that's a good sign.
I suppose you know you're writing the
truth when you're terrified.

poetry

Nobody is saying anything at the
dinner table tonight,
because everyone is too angry.
The only noise is the clinking of
fine silver on bone china and
the sound of other people's children
playing outside
but this will give you poetry.

There is no knife in the kitchen sharp
enough to cut the tension
and your grandmother's hands are
shaking.
The meat and yam stick in your
throat
and you do not dare even to whisper,
please pass the salt,
but this will give you poetry.

Your father is breathing out of his
mouth
he is set to beat the spark out of you
tonight
for reasons he isn't even sure of
himself yet.
You will come away bruised.

You will come away bruised
but this will give you poetry.

The bruising will shatter.
The bruising will shatter into
black diamond.
No one will sit beside you in class.
Maybe your life will work.
Most likely it won't at first
but that
will give you poetry.

wine

It's never too late to be wise.
See how your spirit has been
fermenting.

another thing that happened

We are in the car.
I am screaming at my mother
crying in frustration over her horrible
taste in men,
asking her why she always chooses
the ones who stare at my breasts
through my nightdress
or the ones who steal her money
or cheat or disappear
and this time she doesn't slap me
in the mouth.
She stares ahead, unblinking. Tells me
about her mother's father,
a good-looking man with glinting
eyes and a round face
who followed her into a room when
she was eleven and forced her onto her
back.

We are in the car.
I am somewhere between eight and twenty
and she is somewhere between
nineteen and thirty-five
but I am not completely sure of the
ages. They are melting into each other,
swirling out of reach
because this is a dream, you see, and I

am telling her about the gangly, tall,
awful man that she is with
the one who everyone calls
handsome.
The one who hides food and
tries to walk in on me in the bathtub.

The only conversation that we ever
had about all of this
(the only conversation that actually
really happened)
was when I was thirteen and we were
arguing in the living room
(over the very same man)
and she was going to hit me
and said,
"My grandfather tried to rape me.
Count yourself lucky."

I was stunned into silence. I did not
want to imagine something so terrible
happening
or almost happening to her
and besides, I had already made her a
non-ally.
She wanted to talk. She needed to
talk.
How I wish I had asked even one
question
but it is too late now.
I was too young and

she died young
alone in a hospice while I was living
far away, mostly unavailable.

My mother is with me most nights, though.
She ~~was~~ *is* my first love.
I dream her fiercely
and in those dreams I love her
and get angry and shake her
and bite, grind my teeth
and wake up,
full of everything.

untitled 2

Seize that loveliness.
It has always been yours.

dankyes (Mwaghavul)

Today is the first day
of the rest of it.
Of course there will be other first
days
but none exactly like this.

acknowledgments

nayyirah melissa emilyne rosa
nickque tapiwa
marcia.